HAWAII

A Picture Book to Remember Her by

CRESCENT BOOKS
NEW YORK

CLB 1089
© 1987 Illustrations and text: Colour Library Books Ltd.,
    Guildford, Surrey, England.
Text filmsetting by Acesetters Ltd., Richmond, Surrey, England.
All rights reserved.
Printed and bound in Barcelona. Spain by Cronion, S.A.
1987 edition published by Crescent Books, distributed by Crown Publishers, Inc.
ISBN 0 517 27083 8
h g f e d c b a

The birth of the Hawaiian Islands came some millions of years ago, when volcanic eruptions along the ocean floor produced a great, crescent-shaped chain of mountains. This stretches for 1,500 miles across the Pacific, and its southeastern summits form 'the loveliest fleet of islands that lies anchored in any ocean'. The largest and youngest of these, Hawaii, is still subject to often spectacular volcanic activity from the mountains of Mauna Loa and the constantly seething Kilauea.

The earliest people to come to these islands are thought to have been skilled Polynesian seamen, in about 400 AD. They traveled in huge, double-hulled canoes, 60 to 80 feet long, and brought with them their families, animals, personal belongings and even plants such as taro, bananas, sugar cane and sweet potatoes. They were a stone age people, with a purely oral culture rich in myth and legend, much practical skill in the fashioning of wood, shell, stone and bone, and, apparently, an advanced knowledge of astronomy as an aid to navigation.

The first European to discover this isolated society was the English explorer and navigator, Captain James Cook. He sighted the islands in January 1778 and landed at Waimea on Kauai Island. The islanders believed him to be a reincarnation of the god Lono, whose festival it was at the time of his arrival, and they welcomed him with the traditional Hawaiian reception, known as 'aloha'. Cook encouraged peaceful bartering between his crew and the islanders, exchanging metal objects, something which the Hawaiians had never seen before, for food.

Cook left the islands on 4 February, only to be forced to return to Kealakekua Bay after a sudden storm badly damaged the foremast of the *Resolution*. This time the islanders removed nails and a metal cutter from the ship. The indignant Captain led a party ashore to recover the stolen goods, and in the ensuing struggle was stabbed and clubbed to death at the edge of the bay. His crew buried him at sea with full naval honors.

At this time the islands were separate feudal kingdoms, frequently at war with each other. Then Kamehameha, the nephew of the King of Hawaii, began, with the aid of European military techniques and weapons, to unite the kingdoms under his own determined rule. Entrusted on his uncle's death with the guardianship of the family war god, Kamehameha proceeded to act under his influence and, in 1782, gave battle to the king's rightful successor. By 1791 he was king of Hawaii, and by 1795 had gained control of the majority of the islands. One of his bloodiest battles came in April of that year when he landed his canoes at Waikiki on Oahu. He drove the island's warriors inland until they were trapped at the edge of the steep cliffs of Nuuanu Pali, where many were killed in battle, and the remainder fell to their deaths. The islands of Kauai and Niihau submitted peacefully, and by 1810 Kamehameha was king of all 'the loveliest fleet of islands'.

The dynasty he founded ruled the islands in relative peace for 77 years. During this time the new monarchs welcomed contacts and involvement with the outside world. They promoted the growth of agriculture and encouraged trade, particularly with England, France, Russia and the USA. Initially, the most lucrative trade was in sandalwood, a commodity highly prized in China. The whaling industry, based at Honolulu and Lahaina, thrived, as did trade in the now commercially grown crops of sugar, coffee, rice and pineapples.

New peoples now made the hazardous journey to settle the islands. Chinese, Japanese, and later Filipinos came to work the sugar cane and pineapple plantations. Perhaps the most influential arrivals were missionaries, the first being dedicated New England Protestants who came in 1820 and, in addition to preaching the Gospel, taught the islanders reading, writing and arithmetic. Their teachings did much to undermine the old ways and religion of the islanders, and, though a time of material prosperity, the rule of the Kamahamehas saw the gradual disintegration of much of Hawaii's ancient culture under the onslaught of outside influences.

The monarchy was peacefully overthrown in 1893 and replaced the following year with a republic. Outside influence soon grew into domination when, with the support of the islands' President, the American Congress issued a joint annexation resolution in 1898. This was confirmed on June 14, 1900, when the Hawaiian Islands were established as a territory. The first half of the 20th century saw growth in population, and the development of a modern economy based on the production of sugar and pineapples for export. It also saw the beginning of Hawaii's long struggle for statehood, which was not finally achieved until August 1959, when the islands became the Aloha State, the 50th member of the Union.

Today the Hawaiian Islands are a truly cosmopolitan state. Their population is composed of many races, and every year more visitors are attracted to their shores. The colorful traditions of the original Hawaiian race now continue alongside the most modern of city lifestyles, together with a thriving tourist industry based on the unchanging beauty of the islands.

Traditional Hawaiian costume.

The beauty of Kauai's coastline (these pages) ranges from the harsh rocky shore at Makehuena Point (left), in the south of the island, to palm-shaded Poipu Beach (bottom center) and the resort developments of the Koloa Coast (bottom left).

Right: farmland in the central plantations
near Waimea Canyon, and (inset right) the
slopes of the Hanalei Mountains, Kauai.
Top: fields of sugar cane and (above) taro
plant fields, Kauai.

Facing page: Fern Grotto near Wailua, and (top) Coco
Palms Lagoon, Kauai. Left: child with flower
garlands or leis, and (above) the Church of All
Nations at Lihue, framed by a royal poinciana tree.

Below: sugar cane fields, (bottom right) taro patches bordering the Hanalei River, and (bottom) rich farmland in the Kawaihali District, Kauai. Right: a house amidst colorful vegetation near Kapaa, (below right) the Opaekaa Falls, and (far right) Waimea Canyon, Kauai.

Facing page: (top left)
Barking Sands, and (top
right) white sand beaches,
Kauai. Above and facing page
bottom: Spouting Horn, on
Kauai, where the sea is
forced up, geyser like,
through a lava tube. Left:
folded cliffs on the Na Pali
coast, and (top) the steep
Slippery Slide at Kilauea.

Right: sunset over Ala Moana Park, a favorite recreation
area on the island of Oahu, capital of the Hawaiian
archipelago. Top: the Hilton Rainbow Tower on Waikiki Beach
(above), where thousands of tourists enjoy sunshine, clear
seas and exciting surfing (inset top right).

Facing page: Sunset Beach, where waves can run as high as 30 feet. Above left: the peaceful summer waters of Waimea Bay, Oahu, which come to life in winter, offering demanding sport to expert surfers. Left: a ship and (top left) performing dolphins in Sea Life Park, at Makapuu Point on Oahu.

Above center: rocky, uninhabited Manana Island, situated off the east coast of Oahu. Top and above: the luxurious hotels of Waikiki, where the Ala Wai Yacht Harbor (right) shelters only private yachts.

The white sands of
Waikiki Beach (below) are
dominated by the crater
of Diamond Head (right).
Bottom: the luxury towers
of Waikiki. Facing page:
the *USS Arizona Memorial*,
placed above the
battleship *Arizona*, which
went down with 1,102 men
on board during the
Japanese air attack on
the American Naval base
at Pearl Harbor in 1941.

Vast Kaneohe Bay (left) curves into the east coast of Oahu for eight beautiful miles. Above: Manana Island, also known as Rabbit Island for the population of European hares introduced here by a sugar planter in the 1880s. Manana's other occupants include shearwaters, noddies and terns. Below: the skyscrapers of Waikiki overlook Waikiki Beach, and (far left) modern blocks and the ornate Aloha Tower face Honolulu Harbor on Mamala Bay.

Twin tunnels pierce the Koolau Range (bottom right), which stretches the length of eastern Oahu. Below: the Museum of the Mission Houses in Honolulu. Right: Waikiki Beach, (bottom center) Kihea Beach, and (bottom left) outrigger canoes, Oahu.

Far left and below: the modern face of Honolulu. Left: Waikiki, where green Kapiolani Park backs the white hotel blocks and the fringe of palm trees and golden Waikiki Beach. Bottom left: Waikiki Beach and the dark mass of Diamond Head, formed some 150,000 years ago in a series of undersea volcanic eruptions.

The Mormon Temple (far left) stands in 6,000 acres of land near the town of Laie on Oahu's northeast coast. Above far left: Waikiki, its skyscrapers bordering the Ala Wai Canal and overlooking the Ala Wai Field and Park. Below: one of the Moku Lua Islands, off Oahu's southeast coast, which are now protected as a seabird sanctuary. Above left: Makapuu Beach, (above) surfers on Waikiki Beach, and (left) coconut gathering.

Above: Maili Point and the curve of Ulahawa Beach Park, and (top) mountains in Makua Kaena State Park, Oahu. Left: the replica Byodo-In Temple, in the Ahuimanu Valley of the Koolau Mountains. Inset top left: statue of Kamehameha the Great, who became king of Hawaii Island in 1782, Honolulu.

Bottom: the rocky beach at Kailua Bay, (left) a bright catamaran beaching at Waikiki, and (inset bottom) traditionally colorful Polynesian costume. Inset top: surfing, and (below) a spectacular Hawaiian sunset beyond Waikiki Beach.

Facing page: (top) the grave of Mother Marianne, a former helper at a leper colony on Molokai which was founded by Father Damien in the 19th century, and (bottom right) the house of a guide at the colony. (Bottom left) Kepuki Beach. Left: the Church of Our Lady of Sorrows near Kalauaha. Below: the clouded Pali Coast, which stretches between Kalaupapa and Halawa, Molokai.

Isolated by miles of ocean, the Hawaiian Islands have developed a highly distinctive tropical flora, including (bottom) the rocket protea, (left) the abundant royal poinciana or flame tree and (below left) hibiscus, the state flower of Hawaii.

Right: yachts moored in the harbor of
Lahaina, a former whaling town now
designated a National Historic Landmark,
Maui. Top: Molokini Island, (above center)
Waianapanapa State Park, and (above)
Kahakuloa Head, on Maui's northeast coast.

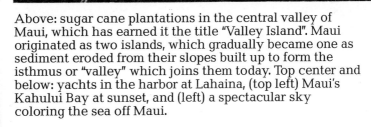

Above: sugar cane plantations in the central valley of Maui, which has earned it the title "Valley Island". Maui originated as two islands, which gradually became one as sediment eroded from their slopes built up to form the isthmus or "valley" which joins them today. Top center and below: yachts in the harbor at Lahaina, (top left) Maui's Kahului Bay at sunset, and (left) a spectacular sky coloring the sea off Maui.

The Lahaina, Kaanapali and Pacific Railroad (right) was built to haul sugar cane from the plantations of Maui. Today, the beautifully-restored turn-of-the-century engines carry only tourists along the six miles of track still in operation. Top center: giant bronze Amitabha Buddha at the Jodo Mission in Maui, erected to mark the hundredth anniversary of the arrival of the first Japanese plantation laborers in 1868. Top right: isolated homes in the hills of Maui. Top and above: fishing boats, for hire to the many who come to Hawaii to enjoy the excellent fishing available off the islands' coasts.

The extremely rare
silversword (above) is
found only on the slopes
of Haleakala, on the
island of Maui. The bush
of silver spikes takes
twenty years to grow,
flowers once and then
dies. Right and far
right: fishing boats and
tackle, and (facing page)
silhouetted coconut
palms.

Renowned for their tropical plants, the Nahi Mau Gardens (center left) cover 30 acres of land on the Waiakea Peninsula of Hawaii. Left: ixora, and (bottom left) water lilies. Far left: stands of bamboo beside a splash pool in Kolekole Park, and (below) green-bordered Mauna Beach, Hawaii Island.

Facing page: valley in
the Hamakua Coast region
of Hawaii. Left: Parker
Ranch, which spreads
across the slopes of
Mauna Kea and the Kohala
Mountains, and (top) a
prosperous house, also in
the pastoral Waimea area
of Hawaii Island. Above:
Kauahaad Congregational
Church, Hawaii Island.

Far left: motorized replica of a triple-hulled Royal Canoe in Kailua Harbor. Top: coral and lava beach of Milolii on the Kona Coast, and (top left) the Hamakua Coast, Hawaii. Left: Mauna Lani Bay Hotel, and (above) Mauna Kea, Hawaii Island.

The City of Refuge, or
Pu'uhonua, (far right) at
Honaunau, was destroyed by
Christian Hawaiians in 1829
as part of their rejection
of the old gods, and has now
been rebuilt as the
showpiece of a National
Historic Park. Carvings
(right) of the old Hawaiian
gods guard the City, once a
haven for fugitives. Below:
lava columns, evidence of
Hawaii's volcanic past.
Bottom: the luxurious
Sheraton-Royal Waikoloa
Hotel, beautifully situated
on the Kohala coast of
Hawaii Island.

Left: the old and the new – a motorized fishing launch passes a traditional outrigger canoe in Kailua Harbor, backed by the steeple of Makuaikaua Church and two-storied Hulihee Palace, Hawaii Island. Completed in 1837 by Hawaii's first missionaries, this church is the oldest in the Islands. Hulihee Palace was built between 1837 and 1838 by Kuakini, the brother of Kamehameha's favorite wife and governor of the island in 1820. Above: the pool at Mauna Lani Bay Hotel, adjacent to the crescent-shaped beach of Makaiwa Bay, and (below) Kaunaoa Bay on Hawaii Island's west coast.

Over 15,000 varieties of orchid (bottom right) may be found growing on Hawaii Island, among them the vanda orchid (below) and the cattleya orchid (facing page). In addition, Hawaiian flora boasts plumeria (center right), much used in the making of leis, the aptly-named candle bush (bottom), and the glory bush (right).

Above: fishing boats moored in Honokohau Harbor, and (top right) a traditional canoe passing the modern hotels of Kailua, one of the largest resorts on Hawaii Island. Top: Kaimu Black Sand Beach, formed when lava hit the sea, shattered and was ground to sand by the surf. Right: St. Peter's Catholic Church, built on the site of an ancient Hawaiian temple, Hawaii Island.

Facing page: Lahaina, once the royal capital of the Hawaiian Islands, and (left) St. Benedict's Catholic church, known as the "Painted Church". Bottom: Kahaluu Beach, and (below) Kaimu Black Sand Beach.

Right and top: palm-tree'd
golf courses, Hawaii Island.
Above: the Kona Surf Resort,
and (inset top right) the
black-rock coast at
Opihikao, one of the oldest
villages in the islands, on
Hawaii Island. Overleaf:
Devastation Trail, a half-
mile boardwalk crossing an
area of black cinders and
skeleton forest created by
volcanic activity in Kilauea
Iki Crater, Hawaii Island.